I0426617

THE AFRICAN ROOTS OF JUMPING THE BROOM

THE AFRICAN ROOTS OF JUMPING THE BROOM

TOLAGBE M. OGUNLEYE

To order additional copies of this book, contact:
Xlibris Corporation
1-888-795-4274
www.Xlibris.com
Orders@Xlibris.com
25444

CONTENTS

I dedicate this book to the memory of my dyaiseuo sister, Nya Ife Olubunmi Montana Manyansa, who made the transition on April 23, 2004. My sister was a wonderful friend and an exceptionally creative, selfless, and loving human being. She was the sixth in our class of eleven sisters, Wudyedema Sifunio 1983 (rites of passage for young women). I will miss her.

This book is also dedicated to those Africans born in America who valiantly strive daily to shape and determine their own realities and destinies.

INTRODUCTION

The aim of this book is to attempt to posthumously bestow value and dignity to the *Jumping the Broom* weddings of enslaved Africans by uncovering this ceremony's African genesis and elements. To accomplish this task, I will dispel the myth of a European and Gypsy origin of this practice by identifying the ancient African nations that existed in the British Isles and then linking them to this ritual. Then I will trace the *Jumping the Broom* wedding to earlier African matrimonial rites and customs that were performed to establish and preserve conjugal unions, protect families, and safeguard homes.[1] I will also delineate the symbols, attributes, functions, acts of veneration, and taboos associated with several deities of Kemet (Egypt)[2] and central and West Africa from which this ceremony derives in order to place *Jumping the Broom* within an African-centered context.

Contrary to the information found in contemporary African American wedding magazines and handbooks, the matrimonial practice known as *Jumping the Broom* has not been documented as ever taking place in Africa. This custom is actually based on the *Besom Wedding* and *Handfasting* traditions that have origins in the British Isles. During the *Ma'afa*, or Holocaust of Enslavement, enslavers from this region of Europe forced innumerable Africans held in captivity to observe the broom jumping segment of these traditions when they were permitted to marry. The recorded testimonies of countless formerly enslaved Africans reveal that most of the enslavers who presided over these ceremonies did not consider *Jumping the Broom* to be meaningful or sacred. Consequently, they performed this rite as though it were a skit in a minstrel show. Assuming roles analogous to the master of ceremonies or interlocutor found in minstrelsy, these captors derisively transformed the couples they purported to "marry" into comical caricatures they subsequently denigrated and exploited. Heckling was commonplace during these ceremonies and ostensibly aimed at not only humiliating enslaved Africans but also propagating racist and stereotypical ideas such as black women's supposed penchant for emasculating black men! Moreover, it was not uncommon for enslavers to sell away from one another the couples they had married according to this tradition. Albeit, enslaved Africans who were married in Christian ceremonies were just as likely to be sold and separated. Despite enslavers' nuptial preferences, all African captives were first and foremost viewed as laborers and investments that could be put up for sale at anytime.

Instances of enslavers' antics and improprieties during and after these *Jumping the Broom Wedding* ceremonies span the entirety of the Holocaust of Enslavement and are just too numerous to mention. However, the testimony of Mrs. Tempie Durham, a formerly enslaved African, is instructive.[3] Mrs. Durham informs us that during her wedding ceremony, George, her captor, wanted "to have his fun." George tells Mrs. Durham and her soon-to-be husband, Mr. Exter Durham, that after jumping over the broomstick forwards, they must also jump over it backwards to determine who is going to be the "boss" of the household. George, the enslaver, grabs a dirty broom that was strewn in the backyard and holds it by its handle horizontally—approximately one foot from the ground. He then instructs the couple to jump forward and backward over the broomstick one at a time. Though Mrs. Durham is able to effortlessly jump both forward and backward over the broom, Mr. Durham—who is inebriated— is unable to clear the broom, and he falls headlong. George, their enslaver, starts laughing uncontrollably and informs the now-married couple that Exter, the husband, will be "bossed till he skeered to speak less'n I tell [sic] him to speak" (Mellon 1990, 146-147).

Although countless negative connotations and degrading acts, such as the aforementioned, typify enslaved Africans' experiences with this matrimonial practice, there exists substantial evidence to prove that this ritual was alien to most of the Europeans who forced enslaved Africans into observing this tradition. Furthermore, it was not Gypsies but, rather, the Africans residing in the British Isles who created these nuptials. The significant components of the *Besom Wedding* and *Handfasting* tradition, from which *Jumping the Broom* derives, originated in Africa. Africans grafted together the elements of the *Besom* and *Handfasting* wedding ceremonies based on their reverence for and adherence to ancient African religious and cultural practices. These components were then formalized into the aforementioned rituals during these Africans' tenure in Europe during antiquity.

The Africans who fashioned these matrimonial practices and populated the isles of the North Atlantic came from countries and empires such as

Ethiopia, Kemet, Kush, Mali, Mauritania, Somalia, Songhai, as well as other areas of the continent. These Africans "did not make a single, sudden trek" into this area of Europe during one particular point in history. Instead, by sea, in successive waves, Africans voyagers, explorers, colonists, tourists, and warriors penetrated the Eurasian continent "from the earliest periods of recorded history and before, down to the recent past" (Luke 1993, 223). The Africans that came traversed, explored, mapped out, named and left an indelible mark on the language, culture, and creed of the entire British Isles long before the invasions of the Romans, Norsemen, and other Europeans. According to Gerald Massey (1884), the effort made by Europeans arriving afterwards "to obliterate the deeper" intellectual, scientific, and cultural imprints made by these earlier African men and women was executed in vain (ibid., 445).

CHAPTER ONE

The Myth of a Gypsy Origin of Jumping the Broom

Although proclaimed in the texts, journals, and magazines of numerous Eurocentric folklorists and contemporary African American wedding planners, Gypsies did not bring the *Besom Wedding* or *Handfasting* tradition to the British Isles in the eighteenth century.[4] Scottish historian, David MacRitchie, argued in his two-volume work entitled *Ancient and Modern Britons* (1994/1884) that no documented evidence exists related to Gypsies arriving in the British Isles during the 1700s. Instead, MacRitchie maintained that the so-called Gypsies who have been labeled as eighteenth-century newcomers were actually natives of Great Britain and the progeny of Africans who had lived there for thousands of years. According to T. Gwynn Jones (1979/1930), attributing this custom to Gypsy origins must be ruled as doubtful because there is no similar marital rite recorded for Gypsies anywhere outside of Great Britain. There are, however, notable parallels in the use of the broom in the ancient wedding customs and religious practices between the Brits and the Danes of Scandinavia—another historical race of Africans.[5]

If there was a notable arrival of Gypsies into Europe during this period of time, as some researchers purport, folklorist Rhy Jones (1928) maintained that their date of arrival was too late to introduce a custom that was widespread throughout Wales for another 160 years. Jones argued, moreover, that *Jumping the Broom* was, at one time, the only form of marriage known among the ancient Celts of the British Isles, and it is more probable that the Gypsies adopted the *Besom Wedding* during their migrations through Ireland, Scotland, England, Manx, and Wales (ibid., 161, 165-166). Barashango (1983) and other researchers argue that the ancient Celts were Africans, and they contend that the appellation "Celt" is actually a corruption of the name Kush, the ancient African civilization from whence the Celts (or Kushites) who settled in the British Isles are believed to have originated.[6]

Rhy Jones also refutes a Gypsy origin of the *Besom Wedding* (referred to as *"Priodas Ysgub"* by the Welsh) based on his comparison of its performance by the people of Wales and the purported British Gypsies. To support his hypothesis, he examined the eighteenth and nineteenth centuries' parish records of Ceirog Valley, Wales, to garner information about broom weddings and the number performed during this two-hundred-year period. Furthermore, he interviewed Welsh citizens throughout the country, whose parents or elderly family members had been wedded by marriage over the *shuvél*, or broom. Jones concluded that the parallels were just too great to attribute a Gypsy origin to this practice. T. W. Thompson (1912) also researched the *Priodas Ysgub* of the Welsh. Like his successor, Thompson determined that the Gypsies acquired the tradition of *Jumping the Broom* from their contact with the indigenous peoples of the British Isles. He stated that in contrast to the centuries that this tradition was performed throughout Wales and other countries of the isles of the North Atlantic, the Gypsies adopted this custom in "comparatively recent times." Thompson asserted, moreover, that in addition to embracing the matrimonial practice known as *Jumping the Broom*, the Gypsies adopted and "helped to disseminate" many of Great Britain's "native tunes, songs and dances, medical recipes, charms and omens" (ibid., 256). Thompson's refutation of a Gypsies origin is significant. However, he does not ponder why the "Gypsies" are extremely knowledgeable of so many aspects of ancient British culture, nor does he consider their motivations for helping to propagate it. He does not reach the same conclusion as MacRitchie—that the Gypsies are conversant with British culture because they are actually natives and the offspring of the ancient African immigrants that created these cultural practices.

Although this wedding tradition was practiced widely throughout the British Isles, it is the Welsh who are generally recognized as being the creators of the *Besom Wedding* and with bringing this tradition to the United States. While this tradition waned in other parts of the islands of the North Atlantic, its practice persisted in Wales well into the late nineteenth century. This ritual's longevity among the Welsh is attributable to the edicts of the ruler King Hywel AP Cadell AP Rhodri, the grandson of King Rhodri the Moor. During the reign of King Hywel Ap Cadell AP Rhodri, an Afro-Welsh ruler, (890-950 CE), all of the ancient legal customs of Wales were systemized so as to preserve them. That the Welsh primarily lived in isolated areas of the countryside during this time period might also have something to do with the survival of the practice of *Jumping the Broom* well into the mid-eighteen hundreds.

Notwithstanding, all over Europe, the Gypsies were an isolated and despised people who were shunned and looked upon with great suspicion for their alleged decadent and roguish lifestyles. Hence, it is inconceivable that the population of the British Isles would embrace such a significant ceremony from a group of people they generally despised, verbally and physically lambasted, and invariably helped to almost totally annihilate. More importantly, by the eighteenth century, the vast majority of Britons were Christians,[7] and the church was involved in a witch-hunt that began in the seventh century—with the legislation of Theodore of Canterbury— to suppress the worship of other gods and to eradicate the remains of what they perceived to be diabolically heathen Druidic practices. Consequently, it is very unlikely that after more than one thousand years of practicing Christianity, the people of the British Isles would adopt a ritual as momentous as a wedding custom that the church and courts refused to recognize and believed to be pagan.

It must be acknowledged, however, that during Christianity's nascency, this religious creed did not appeal to the European masses in the British Isles.[8] Their lack of receptivity to this faith is attributable to the absence of several key spiritual concepts which were elementally characteristic of their former Druidic or traditional African religious beliefs. To captivate the masses and, therefore, gain their membership and devotion to this faith, the church was compelled to mingle large elements of Druidism into their tenets. The resurrection of a messianic Ausar-like figure, the promise of a better life in the hereafter, salvation of the soul and a prominent role of female deities are a few examples of the types of doctrines that were incorporated. Consequently, a so-called neo-paganism developed within Christianity as thinly disguised Druidic worship continued in monasteries, convents, and churches, and the abovementioned African aspects were integrated into Christian canons and its liturgies. In Christianized versions, the ancient gods and goddesses of the islands of the North Atlantic were transformed into saints.[9] For example, the goddess Brigid [10] became St. Brigit, and her husband Ptah[11] was transformed into St. Patrick, a Europeanized version of this Kemetic god (Massey 188/1994, vol. 1). Even the Afro-Britons' anthropomorphous beliefs about the sacred power of animals, trees, and the forces and elements of nature were woven into Christian dogma and practices. To increase membership, the church

developed the practice of having biblical passages read under oak trees—
one of the trees highly revered by the Druids and other religious sects
among the ancient Britons. British, Irish, Scottish, and Welsh legends about
fortuitously obtaining sacred gold and jewels from dragons and macabre
tales about slews of fire-spitting dragons[12] coming at the end of the world
to kill 75 percent of the world's population are also examples of the types
of stories and details that were woven into early Christian scriptures.

To further advance Britons' acceptance of Christianity, supposedly pagan
buildings were converted into churches, monasteries, and convents. Or
these premises were erected on or near sites held sacred to ancient Druidic
deities and their worshippers. Because these structures were well built and
sturdy, Christian leaderships' rationale for preserving them became twofold:
these sites made potential parishioners' acceptance of Christianity more
palatable, and financially, it was a savings for the church. For instance, in
regards to the financial reward merited by using these well-made structures,
Pope Gregory informed Archbishop Augustine, in 601 CE, that he did not
wish to have any heathen buildings destroyed. According to Gregory, those
buildings were too well constructed to be demolished. Instead, the pope
insisted that those structures be transformed from "the worship of demons
to the service of the true god" (Mackenzie 1923, 12). The Christian shrine
of St. Brigit at Kildare, for example, was actually the edifice of a much
older community of druidesses who preserved the sacred fire there, and a
druidical college, in Londonderry, was converted into a monastery (Spence
1949, 57).

Notwithstanding, the name "Gypsy" was used throughout the entire
Eurasian continent to define the peoples living there whose ancestral ties
and social customs could be traced to Kemet and other parts of Africa
(MacRitchie 1994/1884, 1:141). After over thirty generations of
miscegenation or interbreeding, infusing their blood with northern
Europeans, (i.e., the Flemish, Normans, and Scythians), the intensity of
these Africans' resemblances in complexion to the original ancestral stock
had diminished greatly. Yet, the people labeled Gypsies were actually the
descendants of Africans who had come to the British Isles directly from the
African continent from countries such as Ethiopia, Ghana, Kemet,
Mauritania, Nubia, and Somalia, as well as other countries in central,
southern, and western Africa. Others migrated to the British Isles after
living for some time in colonies they or their forebears established in places
such as Arabia, Denmark, India, Persia, and Spain. As late as the mid-

twentieth century, researchers were still describing the complexions of the posterity of these Africans as "deeply pigmented," "being olive, or even darker." Their hair was described as straight and black with a "peculiar kind of blackness" known as blue black, and the irises of their eyes were described as being "dark" with an "indescribable luster" (Thompson 1912, 315). Before the fifteenth-century fall of the seven-hundred-year reigning Moorish Empire, these Africans were greatly esteemed. For tens of thousands of years, they played a major role in the religious, cultural, economic, technical, structural and political development of the islands of the North Atlantic[13].

CHAPTER TWO

Ancient African Britons

The Africans who entered the British Isles during several millennia were most notably called Dammonii, Fomorians, Iberians, Kymyric, Picts, Scots, and Silures. How these names were chosen or given to these Afro-Britons is still debatable. The British Egyptologist, Gerald Massey, believed that their names were derived from the names of the principal goddesses they worshipped, as well as the geographical areas they inhabited in the British Isles. For example, according to Massey, the name Pict denotes the principal goddess these Afro-Britons worshipped as well as their geographic locality. The primary female deity of the Picts was the Kemetic goddess Bast, who was also called goddess "Pasch"[14] or "Pasht" by some of these people (Massey 1994/1881). Bast, who was known as the cat-headed goddess, was revered for the protection she provided to humans against contagious diseases and evil spirits. She was also the goddess of the household, good luck, perfumes, joy, music, and dancing. Like Het Heru,[15] the goddess Bast was often depicted carrying a sistrum and was known as the lady of the red clothes. Emblematically, the color red was very important within the *Besom Wedding* and will be discussed in depth later. Notwithstanding, Bast was also associated with the goddess Tefnut[16] and the Ma'atic principles of truth, justice, order, and cosmic and social harmony. These doctrines were stressed during the *Besom Wedding,* and their importance to a discussion of *Jumping the Broom* will also be discussed at length.

Though the principal goddess of the Picts might have, in fact, been Kemetic, MacRitchie believed that the Picts were originally the Twa people of central Africa and the first African inhabitants of the British Isles. Conversely, Cheikh Anta Diop (1974) and Ishakamusa Barashongo (1983) believed that the earliest inhabitants of the British Isles and other European countries were the Khoisan people, or so-named Grimaldi, of southern

Africa. Archeological evidence of the Khoisan civilization has been unearthed throughout the entire islands of the North Atlantic. Diop (1974) dated the arrival of the Khoisan into Great Britain at approximately 40,000 BCE. And although many Eurocentric scholars are in denial about both the race and origin of these people, they readily insist that the Picts must be considered the first Scottish nation.

As to the name Pict signifying geographical location, Massey argued that the name Pict comes from the Kemetic word "Pekht" and means the hinder or northern part. Within Scotland, the Picts were geographically located in an area that individuals, viewing the world through a European construct, would consider to be the south. However, the Picts viewed their world and existence from an African-centered perspective. Hence, just as the Khamites called the southernmost area of their country upper Kemet, the Picts referred to the southern area of Scotland, where they resided, as being up or the north. Interestingly, this African geographical referencing was not peculiar to the Picts. Massey stated that even in the early twentieth century, when stating their intentions to travel or giving directions, the people of England were still referring to going up as being the south and going down as being the north (Massey 19944/1881, 15).

Similar to a vast number of continental Africans, the Picts were a matrilineal people, and it was the females' ancestral line and social standing that determined their kings' succession to the throne (MacRitchie 1994/ 1884). The Picts are said to be the first to discover the secrets of mining, minerals, and metals. Throughout the British Isles, bronze ornaments and glass beads, reminiscent of their culture, have been discovered in the sites of their former dwellings. The Picts' homes were built partially or wholly underground, arranged in a fashion similar to the layout of Stonehenge, and were called earth houses or beehives. Massey (1994/1881) believed that Stonehenge might have been built by the Picts and dedicated to the goddess Bast (ibid., 1:277). Ultimately, the Picts became the white inhabitants' mythological gnomes, fians, leprechauns, brownies, and fairies (meaning "enchanted") because of their diminutive physiques, warring skills, the hidden locations of their communities, and the manner in which their homes were constructed. The white populace also referred to their dwellings using mythological connotations such as "Fairy Halls" and "Elf Hillocks" (MacRitchie, *Picts* 1890, 50). However, the Picts also built above ground structures such as Dunstanborough Castle and Hadrian's Wall (Mac Ritchie 1890, 67). Hadrian's Wall was erected during the Romans' five-hundred-year occupation of the British Isles and refurbished during the reign of the African emperor of Rome, Septimus Severus.[17]

With the Picts, farming became a way of life in the British Isles, in approximately 3,000 BCE. Moreover, the Picts were known for their megalithic edifices and hieroglyphic writing system called ogham. The writing was normally chiseled into structures made of stone or wood, and its letters were figured around a circle. Palm shoots were also used to form the letters of the ogham alphabet. Ogham is remarkably similar in characters and meanings to the ancient Mande syllabic script of West Africa's Manding people and the alphabetical writing system called nsibidi.[18] Nsibidi is a graphic system that was at one time used extensively by various nations of people of east-central Nigeria (i.e., Igbo, Edo, and Efik peoples) to communicate philosophic ideas and knowledge. Nsibidi is written, drawn, painted, shaped, or carved on various materials such as: bark, metal, masks, and so forth. The Mande script was probably invented around 4,200 BCE, and like nsibidi and its offshoot, ogham, it was written on stone, wood, and dried palm leaves. Mande was used extensively by Khamite, Sumerian, Elamite, and Dravidian merchants, who engaged in the Transsaharan trade with various peoples of West Africa. Notwithstanding, the Gaelic language of the Scottish people is imbued with elements of the ogham writing and language (Spence 1888, 58). And according to Ali and Ali, the grammar and syntactical structure of Gaelic is African as well (1993). Some researchers claim that the name ogham is derived from Ogmios, the god of learning, eloquence, poetry, and inspiration. However, according to Massey, the name the Picts gave to their script (ogham) comes from the Kemetic word *Aukhem* and means "indestructible" (ibid., 1994/1884, 1:256-257).

The Scots were another nation of Africans who settled in the British Isles. Like the Picts, their kingships were determined by matrilineal blood relationships. Initially, the Scots lived primarily in Ireland but ultimately retreated to the area now known as Scotland after the incessant onslaughts of warmongering tribes such as the Scythians, Flemish, and Normans. A few historians and a smaller number of people from Scotland assert that the first great leader and the progenitor of all the kings who ascended to the Scottish throne was an African woman named Scota—arguably the daughter of a Kemetic pharaoh and from whom their ethnic and country name is said to have derived. Some historians say that the Africans who ultimately became known as the Scots went first to Spain and then settled in the British Isles under the leadership of Khamites such as Sensuret I of the Twelfth Dynasty (approximately 1971 BCE), Tuthmoses III of the Eighteenth Dynasty (approximately 1504 BCE), and General Tarharka—decades before he became pharaoh during the Twenty-fifth Dynasty. MacRitchie argued that these blacks dominated Scotland well in to the time of the Saxon kings. As late as the tenth century CE, three of Scotland's provinces were entirely black—though their kings were considered to be the rulers of all of Scotland.

Massey's position differs with regard to the derivation of the name "Scot." He believed that the Scots were named after their principal Kemetic goddess, Sekhmet, the fire goddess. Massey maintains that the name Scot means "illustrious, noble, honorable sons of Sekhmet" (Massey 1994, 467). Sekhmet's name—as indicated by Massey—is derived from the Kemetic word *sekhem* and means "she who is powerful." The goddess Sekhmet was the patron of physicians, priests, and healers and the spiritual mother of the multigenius Imhotep. Like Bast and Het Heru, she was also identified with the color red. She was the goddess of wisdom, sunsets, death, destruction, smallpox, and other pestilence.[19] According to Kemetic mythology, Sekhmet acquired her role as the deity of smallpox and the sun's destructive powers from her predecessor Het Heru, whom the Greeks called Hathor. Kemetic folklore also states that the primeval goddess Sekhmet-Bast divided into two sisters, Sekhmet and Bast.[20] Just as a symbiotic relationship existed between Sekhmet and Bast, strong ties, political alliances, and geographical proximity historically and advantageously existed in the British Isles between the Picts and Scots. But even more importantly, understanding the connections between Bast, Sekhmet, and Het Heru is paramount to understanding and tracing the African roots of the broom wedding ceremony and will be discussed at length later in this book.

The Iberians hailed originally from northwest Africa but settled in Spain for a time before setting up colonies in the British Isles. The Iberians were enterprising sea mariners who engaged in various types of trade along the northern coasts of Scotland, from Spain to Denmark. They began their maritime trading in Europe in approximately 2000 BCE. The religious practices and belief systems of these people greatly influenced the British Isles. The Iberians also designed and significantly influenced Great Britain's monuments and overall architectural style. The Silures and Dammonii were also the descendants of the wealthy Iberian merchants who colonized Spain.[21] Although they resided in areas throughout the isles of the North

Atlantic, they primarily occupied the southwest territories of Britain, especially the isles of Cassterides, which was eventually called Hesperides. When the Romans, under the direction of Julius Caesar, landed in Britain in 55 BCE, the Silures were still residing there. According to Ali and Ali (1993), the Silures were both "culturally and economically isolated" (ibid., 120). They were a sedentary people and mainly animal herders. However, these Africans were heavily involved in the tin industry of the British Isles. Tacitus, a Roman historian of the first century CE, writes of the Silures as having dark skin and kinky hair (Rogers 1967, 196).

The colleges and religious centers of the Druids and Druidesses were housed along the shores in the isles of Cassterides where the Silures and other groupings of the Iberians lived (MacRitchie 1994/1881, 1:41, 44). However, the spiritual centers, educational institutions, and monuments of the Druids could be found throughout Great Britain, as well as India, France, and other areas of the world (Rogers 1967). The Druids were equal in scientific ability and general scholarship to the Kemetic priests who are known for the Mystery System. Actually, it was the African priests who fled Kemet during numerous onslaughts of foreign invaders that founded the Druidic faith. The Druids were a well-defined exclusive priestly caste (both male and female) with subdivisions having different functions: religious, oracular, divination, administrative, and bardic. The study of Druidism consisted of three grades: bard, ovate, and druid. The training received by initiates did not solely consist of the teaching of religious doctrine. Students who attended Druidic institutions were taught the skills needed to become professionals, such as philosophers, scientists, lore masters, teachers, judges, and councilors to kings and queens. In addition to being taught to read and write, the bard was taught to recite the myths, lore, legends, history, and bloodlines of the kings and queens in lands where they resided. The ovate was taught herb lore and "deeper secrets." The druid was the one who was vastly knowledgeable about the tradition and hence became teacher, counselor, and judge. Druids and Druidesses commanded great respect from the individuals and officials they served. Mackenzie (1928) stated that a "king could not address a Druid, until the Druid had first spoken to the king" (ibid., 19).

Many scholars believe that the Kymry also hailed from ancient Kemet and settled primarily in what is now known as Wales. The present-day Welsh still prefer to call themselves Cymric, their country Cymru, and their language Cymraeg. The principal goddess of the Kymry was Ked, whose Kemetic name is Taweret. Taweret (meaning "The Great One") was believed to be the goddess who looked after women throughout their pregnancies and during labor. She also protected the children born to these mothers. Additionally, Taweret was revered for the defense she provided against illnesses, and as such, she is represented in the Kemetic Pyramid Text as the Divine Nurse. While the Khamites depicted her with the legs and paws of a lion, the tail of a crocodile, human breast, and a swollen belly, the people of the British Isles represented Ked as a hippopotamus and, subsequently, a bear. The bear was also an ancient Kemetic symbol and has been associated primarily with the Ainu or Anu people who established colonies in Great Britain, northern Italy, Persia, India, China, and other parts of Asia. Ked often assisted the god Bes in driving away evil spirits, and Bes assisted Ked as she performed her midwife duties. Throughout the British Isles, images or symbols of Ked were occasionally painted on the walls of homes to protect the entire family from intruders.

The Fomorians settled on all the northern islands along the coast of Ireland and across to Scotland and into Norway. In Ireland, their stronghold was Tory Island—on the northwest coast of Ireland. And in Scotland, they established themselves along the west coast. They first came to these areas under the direction of a Sudanese woman named Ceasair, purportedly the granddaughter of Noah of the Old Testament. By sea, Ceasair led a group of fifty women and three men into Ireland. It was about 500 BCE when she left her homeland in the northern section of Meroe Island, crossed into Kemet, and then sailed into Ireland. An account of her journey into the islands of the North Atlantic is chronicled in the following ancient Irish song.

> Forty days of the strenuous journey
> Was Ireland found before the flood.
> Ceasair found it, fair of colour,
> With people of her bright-skinned ship.
> Ceasair, wherefore come she, with fifty-three
> Persons well complexioned.
> Tuesday she set out, harsh the omen,
> From Meroe Island.
> Twenty days from the crooked Caspian Sea
> To the Cimmerian Sea of protection.

Twenty days from Asia Minor sailing
To the glorious Alps.
In eighteen days she came hither,
To the lofty corner of Spain
Thence to noble Ireland,
In a space of nine days from Spain.

(Ali and Ali 1993, 15).

Like the Picts and Scots, the Fomorians were a matrilineal people. Neith, a goddess of the sea, fertility, and war was one of the primary deities of the Fomorians. It is also conceivable that the deities Bes and Sekhmet were two other major gods these Africans of the Sudan brought to the British Isles.[22] The earliest written copies of the *Annals of Ireland* contain the most accurate information about these Africans. Later versions have either removed all references about their arrival and sojourn in Europe or depict them as a menacing force.

Akin to the civilizations located along the Nile, West Africa provided the British Isles with some of its earliest colonists (Luke 1993). Still pending, however, is data reflecting a more precise time of their arrival. MacRitchie argued that West Africans began arriving at some point during the eighth century CE. According to MacRitchie, the Soninke might have been one of the first groups to land. The prevalence during this time period of Soninke social customs in the British Isles and surnames of such as "Maghan" (a title formerly bestowed upon the kings of Ghana) are used by MacRitchie to gauge the era of their appearance in Scotland. Ali and Ali (1993) believe that the proto-Welsh might, in fact, have originated from Mauritania and Mali in West Africa (ibid., 49).

Jumping the Broom can be traced to the aforementioned African pioneers and, conceivably, others. A scrutiny of this matrimonial practice reveals that this custom and its accouterments evolved from the traditions, philosophies, and spiritual beliefs of the aforementioned African peoples, who, as I stated earlier, migrated to the British Isles during a span of several thousand years. Essentially, *Jumping the Broom* represents, commemorates, and preserves significant aspects of these Africans' former ideals, customs, and cosmogonies. It is from these Africans' customs and beliefs regarding the sacredness, commencement, and preservation of marriages and their rigors to ensure the security and comfort of family abodes that we can garner information about the African roots of the *Besom Wedding* and

Handfasting traditions and how the matrimonial practice of *Jumping the Broom* evolved. While the focus of this book is on the African origin of *Jumping the Broom*, it is important to note that there is incontrovertible evidence which shows that not only were these Africans present in the British Isles, they played very significant roles in the development of early European culture. Furthermore, extant in the cultures of the British Isles are names and symbols reminiscent of an ancient African past. Though most modern books ignore the presence of these Africans, scholars such as Massey (1994), MacRitchie (1991/1884), Barashango (1983), and Ali and Ali (1993) maintain that throughout England, Ireland, Manx, Scotland, and Wales are various expressions, traditions, as well as the names of people, rivers, mountains, villages, forests, and important landmarks whose origins and actual meanings can only be explained and understood by examining numerous languages, religious practices, and cultural traditions of Africa. For example, according to Ali and Ali (1993), the town called Cush in Wales is named after the ancient African civilization Kush (ibid., 15), and the Usk River in South Wales is derived from the word for water "essge" or "ussg" of Dogon people (ibid., 100).

CHAPTER THREE

Tree Marriages and Fire Nuptial Rituals:

African Precursors to Jumping the Broom

Through my investigation of the *Besom Wedding* from an African-centered perspective, I have concluded that one of the African practices this ceremony evolved from was the tree marriages of the Twa and Khoisan people of central and southern Africa. Tree marriages, as well as a great variety of other marital rites that were once practiced in the British Isles, though now extinct, can be linked to the Twa and Khoisan people.[23] Tree marriages sprung from these Africans' metaphysical use of trees and its branches, leaves, and roots as well as their veneration of trees—the earliest form of divine worship. These nations of people and other ancient Africans believed that trees were the sacred abode of deities, the sources of ancient wisdom, and the embodiment of potent spiritual essences that influenced human affairs. Long before the erection of temples and statues to the gods, trees were considered to be shrines, and forests were these Africans' sanctuaries. Most continental Africans also identified trees with the departed, and they believed that certain species of trees and foliage signified ancestral vigilance and spiritual return.

In all probability, the Twa and Khoisan practiced tree marriages during their formative years in the British Isles. Tree marriages were conducted to protect both the bride and groom from ill luck and misfortune and were usually performed at the same time the prospective human couple was being joined matrimonially. It was a seer who normally prescribed tree marriages, and according to this diviner's reading and the couple's circumstances, the bride, groom, or both were obliged to marry a tree (Nathaniel Altman 1994, 100). The tree deemed to be sacred and chosen to serve as the bride and/or bridegroom during these occasions was the ash tree.[24] The Twa and Khoisan believed that this tree outlived the gods and brought good luck and protection. They also associated the ash tree with the rising sun and ancestral wisdom and authority. When ritualistically used by the Khoisan and Twa, this tree served as a bond between the dead and the living. The ash tree also symbolized the dawn of new community or the arrival of the founder of a particular clan. This aspect would have made this tree especially meaningful to these Africans during their nascency in the British Isles.

A scrutiny of the culture, history, and lore of the Druids, Picts, and Scots reveals that they also believed that guardian spirits resided within this tree and that ash trees played an essential role in establishing and preserving love and healthy marriages. Hence, it was the wood of this tree that was often used to construct the broom handles used during *Besom Weddings*. Selecting the wood of the ash tree to make the broom handles was not done perchance. Akin to the Twa, Khoisan, and Khamites, the people of the British Isles regarded this tree as their sacred tree of life and, likewise, used it extensively to invoke deities and express their spiritual convictions and practices. Interestingly, the people of the British Isles also associated the ash tree with voyages and the sea. The Scots believed that the ash tree was the primary home of the spirits and that the first woman descended from this tree (Altman 1994, 75). In addition, the Scots regarded the ash tree as the maternal ancestor of all humanity. Similarly, the Picts revered Bast—their principle deity—as the great cat of the ash tree. And the deity Thor, whom the Scots regarded as king of the gods as well as the god of thunder and lightning, considered the ash tree to be his sacred abode. According to Scottish legends, Thor's esteem for the ash tree developed when this tree was struck by lightning yet remained alive. Luke (1993) contends that Thor is a Europeanized archetype of the various storm and thunder gods that have, for ages, existed in Africa (ibid., 235). The Yoruba god Ṣango, the Akan deity Tano, and the Ewe deity Heviosso are all examples of much more ancient gods of thunder and lightning from West Africa whose myths and temperaments are similar to Thor's. Like Thor, they all wield axes and have trees that are sacred to them. To Ṣango and Heviosso, the ayan tree (shea butter tree) is sacred, and the iroko tree is sacred to Tano. According to the lore of these West Africans, like Thor, all of the aforementioned deities chose their particular tree because of its robustness and ability to withstand electrical charges of lightning.[25]

The Britons also considered the ash tree to be the bearer of celestial fruit. Many nations of peoples of the British Isles called the red berries from the ash or rowan tree "luck berries." According to them, these berries contained a concentrated form of the flesh and blood of various deities. Therefore they drank the liquid extracted from the berries of this tree to cure diseases, renew youthfulness, and protect themselves against evil influences. They believed, furthermore, that the red berries contained fire, or the essence of fire, and they aptly called the wine made from the berries of the ash tree "fire water" or "the water of life" (Mackenzie 1923, 181). Massey states (1994/1881) that the name the Britons selected for this tree can be traced to Africa. Throughout the British Isles, the ash tree was also called a rowan tree. The name rowan is derived from the Kemetic word "ruhan" and means a shrine (ibid., 254.). The ancient Khamites also regarded the ash tree as sacred, and like the Twa and Khoisan, they associated this tree with the rising of the sun. Actually, in Medu Neter, the written word for an ash tree is signified with a pictogram of a man praying to invoke the heavens. Also, the Khamites considered the ash tree to be the backbone of Ausar after his dismembered body was reconstructed and set up by his sister/wife Auset. And as a tree of life, the Khamites regarded the ash as symbolic of the treelike nerves that radiate from the spine of the human body.

An examination of the doctrines and mythologies of the practitioners of the Druidic faith in the British Isles indicates that similar to their southern African counterparts, they too probably performed tree marriages at one time. Ceremonies reenacting the marriages between the gods and goddesses of various trees were commonplace among the Druids. Moreover, European classical literature and mythological stories that were appropriated from the Druids support the past performance of tree marriages. For example, in one legend, to make his wife—Hera—jealous, Zeus (the Greek equivalent to the Kemetic god Ammon) publicly announces that he is remarrying. He has his servants dress up a piece of sculpted wood from a felled sacred oak tree to look like a bride. Just as the ceremony for Zeus to marry this figurine is about to get underway, Hera[26] (the Roman equivalent to the Kemetic goddess Het Heru), in a jealous rage, snatches the veil off of the figure to reveal that it is just a piece of wood. When Hera realizes her competition is merely a slab of oak wood, as opposed to a human being, her love for Zeus is fortified.

Oak trees like ash trees were deemed to be the sacred abodes of gods and goddesses and were oftentimes used to make the besoms used in the *Jumping the Broom* ceremony. Oak trees also held great significance to the

Druids and played a salient role in their worship services. According to the Druids, the oak tree represented the soul and moral responsibility. They also venerated the god Zeus in the form of a great oak. It was in the groves of these trees where the druids and druidesses oftentimes conducted their sacred ceremonies. Furthermore, the oak tree was regarded as the marker of sacred spots. And throughout many parts of Europe, the oak tree was regarded as a sacred food-yielding tree. Like the red berries of the ash tree, the oaks' acorns were regarded as luck bringers, and the parasitic plant that grew on the tree was supposed to be even stronger and more influential than the tree itself (Mackenzie 1923, 180). The oak tree also symbolized the male essence or male personification of god.

To date, available studies have not dealt with the possible occurrence of tree marriages in other areas of the African continent during antiquity.[27] Yet, like the Twa and Khoisan, other continental Africans viewed specific trees in their environs as sacrosanct. Among the Asante, for example, akata trees and Osese trees are considered inviolable and must be propitiated. The king's sacred stool ("ohene adwa") and the queen mother's sacred stool ("ohemma adwa") are by tradition carved from Osese trees. These trees are considered to be so holy that before a carver can even touch the trunk or branch that will be carved; he must first make an offering. The Igbo are another example of an African people who view certain trees in their surroundings as sacred. For them, the ofo tree has immense spiritual significance. Many Africans also believed that, metaphysically, trees played an essential role in establishing and preserving marriages and ensuring the security and sanctity of home life. The sacred opẹ (palm tree) of the Yoruba played such a role. At one time, among the Yoruba, dried leaves, stumps and barks of the opẹ, or palm tree, were placed at thresholds or hung above the lintels of their front doors to protect married couples and their families from ill luck and disasters (Lucas 1970, 279). Not to mention, wooden sticks, representative of Qlarosa, the Yoruba's tutelary deity of houses, were hung at the entrances of homes to protect its residents (ibid., 1970, 163). From Ethiopia to Kwazulu-Natal the marula tree is regarded as sacred and treated with the same respect as the ancestors of the people living in these countries. Moreover, there are a wide range of marriage and fertility rituals associated with this tree that date back as far as 10,000 BCE. During antiquity and even in present times, couples exchange wedding vows under this tree. The Zulu call the marula tree the "marriage tree," because it is used as a symbol of fertility and is used in a cleansing ritual before marriage.

While currently nothing more concrete can be used than ancient texts and mythological lore to substantiate the possible occurrence of the ritual of tree marriages in the British Isles, the practice of brides jumping over burning wooden effigies on their wedding day has been established (Altman 1994). Conceivably, this ritual originates from tree marriages and must also be considered to be a precursor to *Jumping the Broom*. This ancient marital custom was equally presumed to bring good luck to the bride and groom and to protect the couple against evil forces and misfortune (ibid., 1994). Afro-Britons believed that fire was a deity who acted as witness during marriage ceremonies. Moreover, jumping over burning wooden effigies was believed to make brides fertile and most certainly combined other beliefs and practices, many of which are still prevalent throughout the African continent: (1) Trees are the abodes of powerful deified ancestors and other numinous spirits.[28] (2) Fire possesses multifarious spiritual and material energies that can be harnessed for purgation. Furthermore, fire is symbolic of good, the female womb, fertility, and the hearth and home. And (3), through ritual performance and invocations, dolls become potent supernatural forces.[29]

The wedding ceremonial practice of leaping over blazing wooden effigies also signified Afro-Britons' homage to African fire and sun goddesses, namely, Auset, Bast, Het Heru, Sekhmet, and Taweret. The roles and statuses of these deities among the Fomorians, Kymry, Iberians, Picts, Scots, and Silures have already been discussed. What has not been stated heretofore is that, ultimately, these African goddesses were transformed into the ubiquitous goddess Brigid, whom the burning effigy and wedding broomstick eventually represented. Brigid, who was also called Brigit (in Ireland), Bridget, Bride (in England and Scotland), Brigando (Gaul), Briginda, Brigiddu, Breed, Brigantia—and other variations of this name—is a composite of all the aforementioned African goddesses (Massey 1994/1881, 467-470). Brigid, whose name means "honor and renown," was also known as Anu, Danu, and ultimately Diana. Moreover, Brigid was a member and descendant of the Tuatha Dé Danann, a pantheon of goddesses and gods who emerged from the Nubian goddess Anu. The Tuatha Dé Danann was master of Druidic lore. During Europe's Middle Ages, throughout the British Isles and other parts of Europe, Brigid ruled over many important spheres of human endeavor. Brigid was oftentimes represented as a doll made of sheaves of oak, cornhusks, or wood. She was a fire goddess, as well as the domestic goddess of marriage, fertility, housekeeping, weaving, broom making, bread making, dairy products, and childbirth. Brigid was also credited with creating the ogham alphabet and was considered to be the supreme muse who inspired poets, writers, and musicians. She was the goddess of merchants, blacksmiths, and mariners as well. Cows and sheep were under her protection, and the health and growth of dandelion plants, bushes, and ash and birch trees were also under her control. Moreover, she controlled the powers of water and fire. Actually, Brigid's lore was appropriated and secularized by Lady Godiva (emanating from the word "Godgifu" meaning "God-given") who rode naked with her entire body painted black on the back of a horse through the streets of London.[30] And among contemporary adherents of so-called ancient pagan practices, Brigid still figures prominently.

CHAPTER FOUR

Africanisms in the Jumping the Broom Wedding Ceremony

At some point, tree marriages and bounding over blazing wooden effigies during marriage ceremonies became extinct and were ostensibly replaced by the *Besom Wedding* ritual. The *Besom Wedding* had a high moral effect on the community. In addition, *Jumping the Broom* was a form of divining or facilitating supernatural access and agency. Originally, a household or utility broom was not used for these ceremonies. It was a branch or bough of a tree or a broom of flowering or dry pods that was used for these occasions. The *Besom Wedding* was formulated based upon a deep respect for women, the African principle of harmony, and the complementary nature of relationships. To marry according to this tradition meant that husbands and wives were coequal partners. The worth and rights of wives were valued. The woman was not the property of the man, and her legal status did not change on account of getting married or bearing children. *Jumping the Broom* denoted and fostered a counterbalance and counter-dependency between the sexes, with both spouses mutually working and sharing responsibilities for the benefit, well-being, and protection of each other as well as their immediate and extended families. If however, the relationship between the wedded couple soured, by jumping back over the broom within a year, the process was reversed, and the marriage was annulled on grounds of incompatibility of temper. The marriage could also be declared invalid if no children were conceived.

According to the findings of Massey (1994), the name these Afro-Britons gave to the *Jumping the Broom Wedding* ceremony, "Besom" (pronounced bizzum), is derived from the Kemetic words "bes" and "sem." In the Kemetic language—called Medu Neter—the word "bes" literally means to "exhibit or proclaim," "to bear," or "to transfer." In Medu Neter, the word "sem" also has several meanings that aptly define the *Besom Wedding*. In Medu Neter the word "sem" means "to conduct a festival," "join together," "assemble," and "combine." "Sem" also denotes the life force and the four pairs of deities who preside over the four corners of the earth.[31] During the *Besom Wedding*, as it was originally performed in the British Isles, not only would members of the community come together to witness this celebration, but the cleric or elder conducting these rites—along with his or her assistants—would invoke and beseech the gods and goddesses who preside over the four corners of the world and the elements of air, earth, fire, water, and other realms to assemble to stand as witnesses and provide guidance and protection to the couples being joined in matrimony.

Undoubtedly, the name besom also represents the attributes of the African deity Bes. Bes was a god of duality. On one hand, he was considered to be the deity of marriages, guardian of homes, and was associated with household pleasures such as good food, music, dancing, relaxation, sexual gratification, and the renewal of men's sexual prowess. Conversely, Bes was considered to be a god of war. He was just as swift to punish the wicked as he was to facilitate family comfort and entertainment. His tambourine, lyre, and harp could be used to entertain, but along with his sword and knives, these musical instruments could also be transformed into weapons and used against evildoers. Bes was also the protector and entertainer of children. He had no temples; rather, figurines of this god were placed near bedroom doors. His image was painted on walls, carved into bedposts, mirrors, the human body and embroidered into pillows. Interestingly, a game played by the Khamites, where the figure of Bes was prominently represented, is considered to be the prototype of *opon ifá*, the trays used in the Yoruba's system of Ifá divination (Lucas 1970, 395). Though Bes—who is also known as Aha and Bisu—became a fairly major deity in ancient Kemet, this god might have been first worshipped in Punt or present-day Somalia.[32] Both men and women painted Bes's image on their bodies for protection, while childless women tattooed his image on their bodies in hopes of becoming fertile. And prostitutes carved the pubic area of their bodies with the image of Bes to provide a degree of defense against venereal diseases. Perusals of the statues that have been unearthed reveal that, like the Twa and Khoisan people, Bes was very short in stature. The veneration of Bes might have started in southern Africa.[33]

The Afro-Britons' use of the broom was thematically related to the broom rituals and religious practices of continental Africans. The broom, or besom, was the most important symbol used during these nuptials. The broom is a very old, widely recognized, and commanding ideograph that evolved from the ancient African practice of ritualistically using branches and twigs from sacred trees to represent the gods and goddesses and their powers. The broom was also symbolic of cosmic and social order and the prescribed laws of nature and African spiritual entities that govern the civil and religious systems of the universe. Likewise, the besom was a contraction of words, metaphors, and ideas of earlier African traditions that signified prospective couples' relationships with society, the universe, and the divine. When used ceremonially, the broom reminded those being joined in matrimony that not only were their vows sacred, but that, metaphysically, gods, goddesses, ancestors, and the forces of nature shaped and impinged upon their unions and existences. As a simulacrum, the broom also reflected the duality of the gods and goddesses that Afro-Britons worshipped, the inevitability of death, the merits of possessing iwàpèlé or good character,[34] the importance of living in harmony with the earth's rhythmic and cyclical forces, and the consequences for failing to adhere to moral codes and taboos.

Like their continental African counterparts, the ancient Africans of the British Isles commonly used brooms, trees, and its boughs as ideograms. Massey (1994/1881) maintained that the meaning of the besom and other ideographs used by the peoples of the British Isles can be discovered through an examination of the symbols and appurtenances used to represent the thoughts, temperaments, and functions of the gods and goddesses of ancient Kemet, central Africa, and other parts of the continent. The studies conducted by Massey (1994/1881) and other researchers reveal that among the Africans of the British Isles, trees, as well as its branches and leaves, were especially utilized ideographically to depict and express ideas and sentiments vis-à-vis their religious and secular lives; albeit, flowers were also significant ideographs. The Druids and other religious diviners, for example, formed twigs into what they called "tree alphabets" or "branch letters" to construct letters and signs (Massey 1994, 83). The British called this system of writing *Bobileth*, or "Tree writing," and in Gaelic, this script was called *Bethluisnion*. This script consisted of thirty-four characters, and each letter of the *Bobileth* alphabet was named after a tree (i.e., beth-birch, luis-the quicken, nion-ash). And palm shoots, which they considered to be sacred, as well as symbols of the tree of life and knowledge, were used to record time and information about the reigns of their royalty and other important periods in their history (Massey 1994, 289). As a matter of fact, residuals of the prior use of trees as ideographs still exist in the English language. The English word "twig," for example, is defined as meaning, "to understand," "grasp the meaning or nature," and "to perceive; observe" (*The Oxford Dictionary and Thesaurus* 1996, 1651). Moreover, the British muse was considered to be the "tree of knowledge" (Massey 1994, 83).[35] Poets throughout the isles of the North Atlantic believed that by holding twigs and branches from trees deemed sacred while reciting and creating their verses, they would receive divine intervention and inspiration. And prophets and diviners believed that branches and twigs from auspicious trees helped them to see hidden things.

Although the *Jumping the Broom Wedding* ceremony has not been documented as occurring anywhere on the African continent, it is important to note that in several regions of Africa, trees and its fronds, and subsequently, brooms were also used ideographically as well as metaphysically. Many West African peoples still believe that the broom is the flywhisk of the gods (Thompson, R. F. 1994, 63). For example, the Yoruba believe that the broom signifies the gods Ifá (Orunmila) and Sòpònná as well as the qualities of unity and strength. When hung over doorsills, the broom becomes the identification mark of Odù (word of God) which prevents evil from entering the home. "In some cases, a 'treated' broom may be placed by the entrance to a compound to trap a burglar or intruder who is expected to pick up the broom and use it to sweep the yard aimlessly until questioned or arrested by the landlord (Ogunleye, Ojo 1983)." As a symbol of Sòpònná, the broom signifies supernatural retribution. According to Babatunde Lawal (2003), the Yoruba word for the utility broom, *igbálé*, can be etymologized as "í" that which, "gba," sweeps, "ile," the floor. However, the Yoruba also call the broom "owò" meaning, "that which commands respect." Lawal states that a popular saying among the Yoruba is "owò ni t'owo," which means, "the broom demands respect" or "respect belongs to the broom." This is probably why the broom is the symbol of Obaluaiye, the small pox deity—one of the most dreaded orişa in the Yoruba pantheon. The broom is also associated with Nana Buluku, (also called Nana Buruku or Nana Bakuu), the mother of Obaluaiye. Lawal contends moreover that "the association of the broom with Obaluaiye and supernatural retribution links Obaluaiye to Şango, the thunderstorm deity who is said to use thunderbolts to punish offenders . . . Not only that, Obaluaiye is associated with the Igunnu-ko, the tall cylindrical cloth mask that the Yoruba borrowed from the Nupe. Igunnu-ko is also associated with smallpox" (ibid., April 15).

Symbolically, at one time, brooms played an integral role in initiating marriages. The Yoruba of southwest Nigeria used brooms extensively and dually to convey ideas about matrimony and their deities. A case in point, as late as the mid-nineteenth century, in some parts of Yorubaland, prospective wives were still sending the palm fronds used to make brooms as àròkó,[36] or ideographic messages, to communicate their acceptance or contemplation of marriage proposals. Among the Èkìtì Yoruba of Èkìtì State Nigeria, for example, when a man wanted to propose to a woman, a messenger would deliver to her an àròkó message made of six cowrie shells tied with black-and-white thread, wrapped inside a palm leaf. This ideographic message implied "I love you. Please marry me."[37] If the woman accepted this proposition, she would send back an àròkó consisting of nine small pieces of broom straw wrapped in a palm leaf. The straw of the broom was made of palm fibers. Analogous to African Britons' notions, the Yoruba considered palm leaves and fibers to be emblems of sacredness.[38] In returning this ideograph to the man who proposed, the woman was figuratively saying, "Your front is good. Your back is good, and I will be with you until the end." If the woman was somewhat interested in the man's proposal but was not sure he would be faithful and she needed further convincing, she would send back three small pieces of broom straw wrapped in a palm leaf (Ogunleye 1999).[39] If the woman completely rejected the proposal of marriage, she would send the man a small piece of charcoal.

Notwithstanding, in the British Isles, during *Besom Wedding* ceremonies, the broom, as a whole, and each of its components was used ideographically to convey deep philosophical information about the African Britons' social values, cosmogonies, and worldviews. As an ideogram, one aspect the broom imparted information about was the gods and goddesses the Africans of the British Isles venerated, communicated with, and relied upon for assistance in living in harmony with their environment. For example, the broom was used to represent Shu and Afro-Britons' reverence for him as the father of all the gods, his role as the divinity in command of the air; wind; and the space between the earth and the sky, as well as his function in maintaining the appropriate levels of thermal heat and biochemical activities in the body. Actually, using a broom to symbolically stand for Shu was not restricted to the *Besom Wedding*. While at sea, for example, African British mariners strapped brooms, symbolic of Shu, to their ship's mast to calm the winds or change its direction. The wedding broom also denoted the goddesses Bast, Het Heru, Sekhmet, and Tawaret and the roles Africans believed these divinities played in sexuality, fecundity, the creation of life, childbirth, motherhood, womanhood, the maintenance of marital devotion, and so forth. For instance, Afro-Britons believed that the goddess Bast played an important role in sexuality and feminine hygiene, while they considered Het Heru to be significant in the production of healthy semen fluid and marital devotion.[40]

The broom also conveyed African Britons' dependence on the aforementioned deities for the protections they provided against deadly infectious diseases. Likewise, it represented these same gods' abilities to mete out appropriate actions and punishments to those who rebelled against Ra[41], defiled Ma'atic principles, and violated prohibitions. When taboos associated with the use, care, maintenance, and disposal of brooms were disregarded, for example, Shu's vengeful side was believed to be responsible for carrying the contagions through the wind that caused outbreaks of smallpox. Similarly, Sekhmet produced smallpox epidemics when those who rebelled against Ra aroused her anger, although, once appeased, her destructive activities would cease (Hopkins 1983). Wooden figurines, possibly representing the goddess Sekhmet, were appeased and enlisted as cures for smallpox in the British Isles. A member of the O'Herleby family in Ballyvorney, County Cork, for example, piously preserved a wooden image of a woman that was used to cure those smitten with smallpox (Spence 1949, 85-86). Also communicated ideographically by means of the broom was the African Brits' fear that if they failed to live according to the edicts of Ma'at[42], on judgment day, Bast would use the sun's fiery flames to eternally burn all offenders.

Smallpox was one of the major pandemics the Africans of the British Isles were concerned with. A whole community could be totally annihilated by an outbreak of this epidemic if its inhabitants engaged in unsanitary practices and risky behaviors. Hence, the people's disquiet over the potentially deadly aspects of brooms was tacitly communicated during these wedding ceremonies as well.[43] The African Britons' anxieties might have stemmed from their remembrances of a probable smallpox epidemic that occurred some time during the Eighteenth Dynasty of Kemet or the untimely death of the Kemetic pharaoh Rameses V, who, in his early thirties, expired from a disease having all the symptoms and appearances of smallpox (Hopkins 1983). Their concern might, in fact, be traced to a contagion, possibly smallpox, which totally ravaged the Parthalonians around 2000

BCE. The Parthalonians had only been in Ireland for thirty years when their total population of nine thousand people died within a week from this plaque (Ali and Ali 1993, 20). The Fomorians and other African Britons were knowledgeable about how to treat and prevent this disease and were able to survive the spread of this outbreak while many of their European counterparts were not. Like other Africans, the Africans of Great Britain believed dirty brooms were the conduits that spread smallpox. Therefore, brooms used in the house were never used to sweep outside and vice versa. Nor were any brooms burned in the family hearth. Instead, all of the townspeople disposed of their worn-out brooms during the annual Festival of Fire, which occurred during the summer solstice (Massey 1994/1881, 124). This is also probably why it was customary for brooms to be laid aslant in doorways of the abodes where these *Besom Weddings* took place. At the culmination of these ceremonies, the marrying couples jumped over the broom into these homes. Traditionally these weddings took place in the homes bridegrooms built for their brides.

The Africans of the British Isles were not the only Africans to be concerned with the eradication of smallpox, the devastation this disease caused, or to represent Shu's, Bast's, and Sekhmet's reverencing, moralizing, and avenging sides by means of a broom.[44] The Yoruba also used a broom to symbolize Shu, Bast, Het Heru, and Sekhmet. According to the philologist J. Olumide Lucas, Sòpònná, the Yoruba god of smallpox, is, in fact, an amalgam of the Kemetic deities Shu and Het Heru. And apparently, like the ancient Khamites, the Yoruba amalgamated Het Heru with Bast and Sekhmet. Lucas's (1948, 1970) argument stemmed from his extensive research of Yoruba culture and the traditions of other present-day West African peoples. He maintained that the earliest ancestors of the Yoruba— and the majority of other West African peoples—once resided in ancient Kemet and other countries along the Nile Valley. Lucas vociferously argued that when the Yoruba settled in West Africa, their prior social customs, religious beliefs, languages, writing systems, and communication strategies remained relatively unchanged. Moreover, with minor adjustments in names and attributes, their former deities such as Ausar, Auset, Bes, Het Heru, Mut, Ptah, Ra, Set, Shu, and so forth continued to be worshipped. To substantiate his claim, Lucas points out that like Shu, Sòpònná, whom the Yoruba call Obaluaiye, and other variations of this name, is also considered to be king of all the gods and the world. He asserts furthermore that Sòpònná, akin to Shu, is the most dreaded and yet respected god, because of his ability to annihilate. Like Shu, Obaluaiye uses smallpox to punish those who transgress the moral code. Throughout Yorubaland and the African Diaspora, not only is Sòpònná's rancorous side symbolically represented as a broom, but during ceremonies that pay homage to him, his priests and priestesses dress in attire sewn to resemble a broom that is made of raffia straw.

The oral and written history of the Yoruba's prohibitions with regards to brooms supports Lucas's theories. Just as newly married couples in the British Isles were, at one time, formally apprised of the proscriptions they had to adhere related to brooms, the taboos that were imposed on the Yoruba connected to the *ígbálé* were communicated by the *aláwiyè*.[45] These proscriptions can be found in the Yoruba's text of ancient wisdom entitled *Awǫn Eewǫ Ilę̀ Yoruba*, which is translated as *The Book of Don'ts*.[46] In this document, the proper care, usage, disposal, and taboos associated with brooms are outlined, and Sòpònná's representation as an *ǫ̀wǫ̀* or *ígbálé* is discussed at length. Sòpònná's relationship with Het Heru and Het Heru's interrelationship with her predecessor and successor (Sekhmet and Bast) is alluded to (ibid., 70-73). From the *Awǫn Eewǫ Ilę̀ Yoruba*, we can surmise that similar to the Khamites who represented Shu, Bast, Sekhmet and Het Heru as cats, the Yoruba also represented these deities as felines. Not to mention, like Bast, Het Heru, and Sekhmet, cats are the sacred animals of Sòpònná. As the *aláwiyè* had orally transmitted the information in delineating the taboos associated with brooms, *The Book of Don'ts* cautions its readers to be extremely kind to cats, never to beat them with brooms, and to be ever cognizant of Sòpònná's special relationship with and dependency on them. This document also reveals that the Yoruba's veneration for cats and the official measures taken to protect them is remarkably similar to those of the Khamites. In ancient Kemet, cats were greatly esteemed for their connections with the deities, their character, role played in hunting waterfowl, and adeptness at killing snakes and vermin. Cats' adroitness at exterminating rodents consequently led to the protection of their stored foodstuffs and the control of the spread of communicable and deadly diseases. Because of their value, the Khamites enacted stringent laws to protect them. Individuals who failed to abide by the edicts related to the protection of these felines were punished, sometimes quite severely. Furthermore, relative to Lucas's premise that the Yoruba language is a derivative of Medu Neter, it is interesting to note that the Yoruba word for cat, "*ese*," is a modified form of the Kemetic names for cats "bes" and "bessat."

At one time in the British Isles, cats were also cherished and admired for their hygiene, strong mothering instincts, correlations with several male and female deities, ability to retrieve birds for hunters, usefulness in protecting harvested grain, and reducing the spread of diseases by killing mice and other rodents. The ancient Britons also believed that cats brought good luck to marriages. And like the Kemetic god Ptah, St. Patrick was also, at one time, identified with cats. However, cats lost their standing in the British Isles with the arrival of Christianity and this church's one-thousand-year religious campaign to destroy all remnants of the cultural other. Christians associated cats with heathenism, Satan, and witchcraft and began a crusade to exterminate them en masse. Not until after the cat population had been almost totally decimated and the bubonic plague, or Black Death, ravaged Europe—claiming the lives of almost one-third of Europe's population—did Christians finally realize the worth of the cats that had been in their midst and the significant role they had played among the African British in abating the spread of diseases. The killing of cats ceased for a time; however, the Christians' appreciation of cats was short-lived. Not long after the bubonic plague had been arrested, the church's persecution of cats resumed—especially with regard to black cats. In Great Britain, when witch finders sent women who were perceived to be witches to the gallows to be burned or hanged, cats were oftentimes murdered alongside these females!

CHAPTER FIVE

The African Ideographical Signification of the

Wedding Broom's Parts

The handle, brush, and binding of the broom could each be read individually as ideographs symbolic of various aspects of the African axiology and cosmology. The handle or hilt represented the groom (masculine), and the brush or bristles represented the bride (feminine). Moreover, as the Kemetic god Ra is traditionally represented carrying a staff, in all probability, the hilt of the broom also represented the soul of the god Ra. The Yoruba also worship Ra, and they call the stave that represents him "Re Ukhure." Given the myths and legends surrounding the so-called leprechauns and other little people of the British Isles and their connections to the god Ra and other deities of the Tuatha Dé Danann, it is attention-grabbing to consider their correlations to the Yoruba religion and folklore as well. According to Lucas (1948), the Yoruba word "kure-kure"—meaning a fairy, elf, or hobgoblin—is derived from the word "Ukhure," which means the staff of Ra (ibid., 302). Notwithstanding, traditionally, the broom used during the *Besom Wedding* was made by tying twigs of birch around a handle made of ash wood.[47] This combination denoted the life force inherent in all living things and the command the deities that control the four elements—air, earth, fire, and water—have over heaven and the world. The twigs of birch used to make the brush also represented the deity Djehuti—whom the Yoruba call Ifá—and the role they believed he played in establishing law and order and overseeing the four elements. As Djehuti is the god of writing and identified with the birch tree, it is interesting to note that the Africans of the British Isles used the pulp of birch wood to make paper. The peoples of the British Isles also associated the birch tree with Druidic training, the goddess Sekhmet, their ancestors, the start of a new calendar year, and fresh beginnings. Actually, the first letter of the ogham alphabet is the letter *B* for the birch tree. The Druids believed that the birch tree was the link between life and death.

The ancient Africans of the British Isles believed that when the birch tree was used ceremonially, it attracted the powers needed for fertility, protection, purification, and exorcism. During the annual May Day harvest celebration, they decorated birch trees with red-and-white cloths to invoke the powers for fecundity. Joyous eating, drinking, and dancing characterized this festival. The Jack-in-the-Green, a man entirely hidden in a covering of green foliage, danced through the streets on May Day (Evans-Wentz 1911 436). Masqueraded men dancing as the Jack-in-the-Green could be witnessed throughout the entire British Isles on May Day, and they all represented an ancient African agricultural deity. A folk dance was also performed during this May Day celebration which is now called the Moorish dance. Eurocentric scholars want us to believe that the name of this dance, "Moorish," is derived from the word "mores," and hence, the name "Moorish" means that the dance is very old. However, the name is derived from the African men and women who traditionally performed this dance. A dance around the Maypole was also performed during this harvest festival. Massey argued (1994/1881) that the red-and-white cloth which decorated the birch tree that was called a "Maypole" represented the Kemetic deity Ausar.[48] Ausar was the god of vegetation and the creator of agricultural implements,[49] hence his association with the Maypole and the harvest festival.

Ausar has numerous parallels to the Yoruba deity, Oko, as well as the British King Arthur of the Knights of the Round Table. The deities Ausar and Oko are both associated with agriculture, the harvest, and farming tools. The colors of Ausar, Oko, and Arthur are mutually red and white. In regard to Ausar and Arthur, aside from the apparent linguistic similarities in their names, some of their shared features are: Both were monarchs and gods of a mystical cult. Similar to Ausar, King Arthur is regarded as a sun-god incarnate in a human body who teaches arts and sciences and hidden things. Both Ausar and King Arthur had to periodically take journeys to the underworld to subdue evil and learn additional secrets and rites of their sects. Both were associated with the cult of the bull. Furthermore, like Ausar, Arthur promises to return from the dead to defend his nation. Ausar pledges to return to save the world while Arthur swears to come back to rescue Britain when a crisis occurs. Each were betrayed and killed by a close relative. Ausar is murdered by his brother Set who scatters the pieces of his body throughout Kemet, and Arthur's nephew/son named Mordred fatally stabs him at the battle of Camelon. Both men were rescued by their wives who were also their sisters. Ausar's dismembered body is reconstructed by his wife and sister, Auset. Auset uses words of power taught to her by her father, Djehuti, to raise Ausar from the dead and restore him to his kingship. Auset takes Ausar across the Nile to rule in Aalu, a land with plenteous fruit and grain. By boat Morgan le Fay spirits away her husband and brother, Arthur, to the enchanted isle of Avalon. In Avalon, Morgan le Fay nurses Arthur back to life, and his wounds heal (Spence, 1928).

The binding tied around the brooms used for the *Besom Wedding* ceremony symbolized the ankh. As a representation of the African ankh, the binding signified the sacred vows made between husbands and wives and their ability to create life. This cording also signified prospective couples' hopes for long lives together, strength, and good health. According to Massey, the ankh was symbolic of the goddess Neith—a Sudanese, predynastic Kemet, androgynous being—who was the first to be associated with the ankh and its signification to marital bonds and the complementary nature of the male and female principles (ibid. 1994, 14). Neith, whose worship can be traced back to at least 4000 BCE, is called the "Great Mother" and is represented as a white vulture. In her anthropomorphic manifestation, she appears wearing a red crown. In Wales, the wedding breakfast which completed the *Besom Wedding* was referred to as the "Neithor" (R. W. Jones 1979/1930, 159). It is apparent that this banquet paid homage to the goddess Neith! Massey contended, moreover, that the ankh's importance as a symbol of covenants and marital commitment is reminiscent in the expression "tying the knot." Over time, however, the wedding ring replaced the ankh as a symbol of unity, holiness, and marital devotion (Massey 1994/1881, 337).

Red ribbon was decidedly used as the binding that was tied around the besom. As an ideograph, the red ribbon was multisymbolic. The British considered red to be the color of motherhood and life. It denoted the blood of the deities and the source or the beginning. It also signified potentiality and the complex spiritual power that makes things happen.[50] The red ribbon was also symbolic of red ochre—a compound made of iron ore—which the Africans of the British Isles smeared on their bodies as a sign of men's vitality. Also, the color red symbolized the perforation of the hymen and soon-to-be married couples' hopes for sexual vivacity and undying passionate unions. The word power of the Kemetic goddess

Nekhebet and her function in motherhood and maintaining open and continuous communication between husbands and wives was also symbolized by the color red. Additionally, the red ribbon was used in remembrance of the Afro-Britons' dead, who were ritualistically painted or sprinkled with red ochre during their funeral rites. For some of their departed, a form of mummification was performed. The flesh was removed from the deceased person's body, and the bones were stained red. This practice was based on their belief in reincarnation and their views that when the dead were revivified, the bones from the corpses of their former lives would provide the structural framework for their new bodies. Red ribbon was also representative of this color's benefits in curing smallpox.

Aside from the color red being used to symbolize Nekhebet, like Neith, a vulture was also used to represent this goddess. Based on their observations of the life of a vulture, most Africans aspired to mimic these creatures in terms of their motherly aspects, fidelity to their spouses, bonding with and commitment to their chosen partner, and monogamous relationship with that mate.[51] In Great Britain, ultimately, Nekhebet's name was changed to Morrigan. Although Morrigan means "the Black Goddess," many Eurocentric scholars are unwilling to acknowledge that this goddess originated in Africa. Like Brigid, Morrigan subsumed the attributes of numerous female deities. Neith is one of the goddesses that Morrigan assumed. Similar to numerous African goddesses of motherhood, Morrigan was initially symbolized as a vulture. In the isles of the North Atlantic, eventually, she became the symbol of a raven or carrion crow hovering overhead, protecting soldiers during battle.[52] In the Cuchullin stories, Morrigan, like Het Heru, appears with a supernatural cow whose milk heals wounds and prolongs life.

The candles that were traditionally used in this ceremony were symbolic of Brigid and the Eye of Horus. Candles were used "to show, explain, or reveal" (Massey 1994/1881, 290). The circle and the counterclockwise movements that customarily occurred within this ritual represented living in harmony with earth's rhythmic and cyclical manifestations. The circle also represented Stonehenge and the movement of the earth and other planetary constellations. The flowers were symbolic of the sexual properties of the Egyptian lotus and this plant's significance to fecundity. The head of the lotus flower represented Het Heru and her role as the personification of love, beauty, and fertility. The stalk of the lotus, on the other hand, represented creation and reproduction.[53] Though flowers continue to be used in present-day wedding ceremonies, their intended historical meaning has long been forgotten.

Traditionally, in some areas of the British Isles, the act of jumping over the broom was, in fact, the culmination to or solidification of the *Handfasting* wedding ceremony. During the *Handfasting* ceremony, the couple's hands were actually bound together. This is where the expression "joining hands in matrimony" comes from. The pair marrying would vow to stay together for as short as a term of nine months and as long as several lifetimes. It was the couples that believed in reincarnation that would vow to stay together for several lifetimes. After making these pledges of commitment before their gods, goddesses, ancestors, families, and the forces of nature, the bride and groom would then leap over a utility broom—or a bough or twig from the ash, birch, or oak tree—hand in hand.

Ancient African Courtship Practices in the Islands of the Atlantic

Even the contemporary courtship practices of the British Isles can be traced to ancient African beliefs, languages, and customs. For example, during All Hallow Eve in Wales, Welsh youth of both sexes would search for a sprig of ash that was perfectly even-leaved. The first male and female to each find a sprig of ash that was even-leaved would yell out "Cyniver." Based on this discovery, these two youth were supposedly destined to become husband and wife (Massey 1994/1884). Massey stated that the word "cyniver" is a derivative of the Kemetic word "Nefer" and means "good," "beautiful," "perfect," "a crown," "the youth," "puberty," and "to bless" (ibid. 1994/1881, 291). Similarly, Lucas (1948) states that the Yoruba word for good, "ifá," is derived from the Kemetic word "Nefer." Moreover, at one time in the British Isles, when men would propose, they would take their intendeds to a location where a mill, stream, and trees converged— all three were all considered to be symbols of strength and endurance. In Africa, the areas where streams or rivers and forests converge are considered to be the sacred homes of the deities. After presenting a gift of freshly churned butter on a newly made dish, the man would propose saying, "Oh, woman, loved by me, mayst thou give thy heart, thy soul and body." Moreover, to solidify their engagements, couples would join fingers through the opening of a pillar inscribed with sacred ogham writing found in locations such as Kimalocheader Church near Dingle, Co. Kerry, which was built in the seventh century CE (Haggerty 2000).

CHAPTER SIX

Devaluation and Corruption of the Besom Wedding

In the fifteenth century CE, when the Africans of the British Isles lost their social standing, the ancient meaning of the *Besom Wedding* was forgotten, and the white majority discarded the merits of this custom. Discriminatory practices against the Africans of Great Britain coincide with the downfall of the Moorish empire in the late fifteenth century. From this point onward, race hatred toward these Africans began. They were disrespected, persecuted, and their way of life was outlawed. A significant number of these so-called Gypsies were transshipped to the Americas and enslaved during the *Ma'afa.* Many were annihilated. Others were expelled from the districts and territories they had once controlled. Because their castles, homes, and lands were confiscated, they became nomads. By necessity, they were forced to relocate their settlements in proximity to the wastelands, so that when under siege, they could quickly retreat to these barren areas. One of the dire consequences of being nomadic was that changes had to be made in their cultural practices. For example, whereas their families had, at one time, elaborately buried their dead in decorated funerary furniture, vases, and coffins made of sycamore wood,[54] these Africans were now forced to cremate their loved ones—in order to easily take their remains along in small urns as they fled.

Actually, the enslavers who vulgarized the ritual of *Jumping the Broom* brought their contempt for this custom with them from the British Isles. The whites that became enslavers in the United States were still in Europe and yet to be born when their forebears usurped control over the areas of the British Isles that had been formerly possessed by its African inhabitants. These enslavers watched and possibly participated in the denigration of Great Britain's African population. They heard or actually hurled scornful epithets such as "gypsy," "thief," "beggar," "nomad," "felon," "rouge" "ruffian," and "black wench," or *dubh-chaile,* at these Africans (Mac Ritchie n.d.,1:135). Before departing for America, enslavers observed as some of these Africans were sold into slavery while they saw others being consigned to menial and dangerous jobs or reduced to castes of wandering minstrels, mountebanks, fortunetellers, clowns, and buffoons throughout Great Britain. They were trained to use all words and phrases containing the word "black" or associated with the culture of African people as negative expressions (Mac Ritchie 1994/1881, 1:136). Many of the enslavers who came to the United States witnessed broom marriages lose their validity throughout the British Isles, and they heard the language associated with this custom lose its value as well. For example, the word "besom," once a name signifying something honorable and sacred, became a term of contempt towards females. The nomenclature "besom" became a term used to describe a loose or slovenly woman or a busybody. The broom became symbolic with witches, henpecked husbands, and the transfer of power from the male to an emasculating female (Massey 1994/1884, 125). The ash tree that was once considered the haven of gods and goddesses was, during the centuries of the Inquisition and Holocaust of Enslavement, associated with witches' brooms, witchcraft, and evil spells. The dissolution of the *Besom Wedding* signaled the devaluation of the roles played by women in British society and an end to matrilineal lines of descent. This ending also represents the onset of social stratification and hierarchal structures based on men seizing essentially all the power and dominating women. The African Picts became the "Pikey," and, ultimately, the name "Pikey" became the epithet "picaninny" that enslavers disparagingly spewed at the Africans they held in captivity in America.

In the United States enslavers performed and concocted jumping-the-broom routines that had very little resemblance to the manner in which *Besom Wedding* ceremonies were originally conducted in the British Isles. Most enslavers in America were blissfully ignorant of this ritual's formalities and symbolism and, hence, were incapable of performing these ceremonies in a dignified manner as the Druid priests and priestesses had done in Great Britain. Jumping over the broom forward and backward without touching it had nothing whatsoever to do with determining who would be the boss of the household. According to Massey (1994/1881), attempting to jump over the broom without touching it was a form of divining. To step over the broom without touching it meant to be lucky and fortunate. Fortunate in marriage always meant bearing children (ibid., 1:252). Furthermore, couples jumping over the broom together or one at a time signified working together and the complementary nature of marital relationships. What one partner may not be able to provide or do, the other partner can.

Cultural practices of the Africans that were not demonized and denigrated were appropriated. The game of chess, the kilts traditionally worn by men, and the Moorish dance—England's national dance—are just a few of the cultural practices that were commandeered. Many of the last names African Americans inherited from their enslaved ancestors that we believe to be European names were initially the exclusive surnames of Africans who lived in the British Isles and Scandinavia. The Europeans who bear these names have no idea that they carry the names of ancient Africans. To avenge enslaved Africans, I would like to list some of those names here: Brown, Campbell, Carr, Douglas, Duffy, Fall, Falkirk, Gordon, Graham, Grey, Grimes, Jenkins, Kennedy, McLeod, McCray, Mcduff, McPherson, McNabb, Watkins, Wilson, Wright, and Young (Mac Ritchie, 1994/1881, 1:124, 131). Then, of course, there are the names that are derivatives of the name Moor such as: March, Moreland, Morgan, Morris, Morrow, and Morton.

At some point in time, respected elderly enslaved Africans began officiating over a number of *Jumping the Broom* wedding ceremonies on their respective plantations. The elderly enslaved Africans who presided over these ceremonies treated this custom as an honored religious rite, and they showed respect for the couples they were marrying according to this tradition (Brown, W. 1968, 46). In actuality, what enslaved Africans had was far more superior to the other European wedding ceremonies that were performed during the Holocaust of Enslavement. Unbeknownst to enslaved Africans, they were engaging in a wedding custom that connected them to many ancient African peoples and an African cosmology. Despite enslavers' mean-spirited attempts to humiliate the Africans they held captive and defile their sacred unions, unknowingly, these despots provided them with an opportunity to take part in an honorable ritual that stressed love, complementarity, and marital devotion and invoked the same gods, goddesses, and energies that the ancient Africans of the British Isles and the African continent had summoned for millennia.

REFERENCES

Ali, Ahmed, and Ibraham Ali. 1993. *The black Celts*. Wales: Punite Publications.

Altman, Nathaniel. 1994. *Sacred trees*. Sierra Club Books

Abimbola, Wande. 1996. The concept of good character in Ifá literary corpus. *African intellectual heritage: A book of sources*, edited by Molefi Kete Asante and Abu S. Abarry. Philadelphia, PA.: Temple University Press.

Barashango, Ishakamusa. 1983. *African people and European holidays: A mental genocide*. Silver Spring, MD: IVth Dynasty Publishing Company.

Brown, William Wells. 1968. *My southern home*. Upper Saddle River, NJ: Gregg Press.

Buckley, Anthony D. The god of smallpox: Aspects of Yoruba religious knowledge. *Africa,* vol. 55, no. 2:187-200.

Cole, Harriet. 1993. *Jumping the broom: The African-American wedding planner*. New York: Henry Holt & Company.

Churchward, Albert. 1913. *Signs and symbols of primordial man*. New York: George Allen Press.

Davidson, Ellis H. R. 1988. *Myths and symbols in pagan Europe*. Manchester: Manchester University Press.

Diop, Cheikh Anta. 1974. *The African origin of civilization, myth, or reality*. Westport: Lawrence Hill and Company.

Dundes, Alan. 1996. Jumping the broom: On the origin and meaning of an African American wedding custom. *Journal of American Folklore* 109 (summer), no. 433:324-329.

Evans-Wentz, W.Y. 1911. *The fairy-faith in Celtic countries*. London and New York: H. Froude.

Frazier, James G. 1981. *The golden bough: The roots of religion and folklore*. Originally published in 1890 in two volumes. New York: Avenel Books.

Green, Danita Roundtree. 1992. *Broom jumping: A celebration of love*. Richmond, VA.: Entertaining Ideas, Ltd.

Gupta, Sankar Sen, ed. 1965. *Tree symbol worship in India*. Calcutta: Indian Publications.

Haggerty, Bridget. 2000. *The traditional Irish wedding*. UK.: Irish Books and Media Inc.

Hopkins, Donald R. 1983. *Princes and peasants: Smallpox in history*. Chicago and London: University of Chicago Press.

Jones, Rhys W. [1928] 1969. *Besom wedding* in the Ceiriog Valley. *Folklore*. Reprint, London: Nendeln/Liechtenstein.

Jones, T. Gwynn. 1979. *Welsh folklore and folk-custom*. Originally published in 1930. Totowa, NJ: Rowman and Littlefield.

Idowu, Bolaji. 1962. *Olódùmarè, God in Yoruba belief*. Longman, Nigeria.

Lawal, Babatunde. Interview by Tolagbe M. Ogunleye, email correspondence, April 15, 2003.

Lucas, J. Olumide. 1948. *The religion of the Yoruba*. Lagos, Nigeria: CMS Bookshop.

_____. 1970. *Religions in West Africa and ancient Egypt*. Lagos, Nigeria.

Luke, Don. 1993. African presence in the early history of the British Isles and Scandinavia. *African presence in early Europe,* edited by Ivan Van Sertima., New Brunswick, U.S.A., and London, U.K.: Transaction Publishers.

Lurker, Manfred. 1980. *The gods and symbols of ancient Egypt.* N.p.: Thames and Hudson L.T.D. London Inc.

Mackenzie, Donald. 1923. *Ancient man in Britain.* New York: Frederick A. Stokes Company.

Mackenzie, Donald. 1928. *Buddhism in pre-Christian Britain.* London and Glasgow: Blackie & Son Limited.

MacRitchie, David. 1890. *The testimony of tradition.* N.p.: KEGAN PAUL, TRENCH, TRÜBNER & CO., Limited.

_____. 1991. *Ancient and modern Britons.* Vol. 1. Originally published in1884. Freeman S. Dak, U.S.A.: Pine Hill Press, Inc.

_____. 1991. *Ancient and modern Britons.* Vol. 2 Originally published in1884. Freeman S. Dak U.S.A.: Pine Hill Press, Inc.

Massey, Gerald. 1994. *Book of beginnings, Egyptian origines in the British Isles.* Book 1 19. Brooklyn, New York: A & B Book Publishers.

Mellon, James, ed. 1990. *Bullwhip days, the slaves remember.* New York: Avon Books, New York.

Ogunleye, Tolagbe M. 1999. *Àròkó and Ogede*: Yoruba arts and resistance to enslavement in 18th and 19th century Florida. Paper presented at the Conference of Yoruba Culture and Ethics, U.C.L.A., on February, at Los Angeles, California.

Parrinder, Geoffrey. 1963. *Witchcraft: European and African.* London: Faber and Faber.

Philpot, J. H. 1994. *The sacred tree or the tree in religion and myth.* Felinfach: Llanerch Publishers, 1897. Facsimile reprint.

Rogers, Joel. A. 1967. *Sex and race*. Vol. 1. Helga M. Rogers, New York, NY.

Spence, Lewis. 1928. *The mysteries of Britain or the secret rites and traditions of ancient Britain restored*. Philadelphia: David McKay Company

Spence, Lewis. 1949. *The history and origins of Druidism*. New York: Barnes and Noble Inc.

Sullivan, C.W. 1991. Jumping the broom: A further consideration of the origins of an African American wedding custom. *Journal of American Folklore*, vol. 110:203-204.

Thompson, R. F. 1984. *Flash of spirit*. New York: Vintage Books, a division of Random House.

Thompson, T. W. 1913. The ceremonial customs of the British Gipsies. *Folk-Lore* 24: 314-356.

Thorpe, C. O. 1967. *Awǫn Eewǫ Ilẹ́ Yoruba*. Ibadan, Nigeria: Onibon-Oje Press.

Tyldesley, Joyce. 1994. *Daughters of Isis, women in ancient Egypt*. N.p.: Penguin Books.

Verger, Pierre. 1970. *Notes Sur Le Culte Des Oriᵃa Et Vodun*. Originally published in 1957. Amsterdam: Swets & Zeitlinger N.V.

Williams, Chancellor. 1987. *The destruction of black civilization*. Chicago, Illinois: Third World Press.

State of Virginia. 1940. Work Projects Administration. *The Negro in Virginia*. Compiled by the Workers of the Writers Program. New York: Hastings House Publishers.

ENDNOTES

1   The marriage ceremony was continental Africans' first effort to establish a religious rite.

2   Kemet is the ancient name of the country now referred to as Egypt. According to Chancellor Williams (1987), "Aigyptos," or "Egypt," is the name the Greeks unwittingly gave to Kemet. The Greeks derived the name Egypt from the Kemetic word "Hikuptah," the second name of the city of Menes. Hikuptah means "Mansion of the Soul of Ptah." Ptah was a major deity of both upper and lower Kemet. The city of Menes (Memphis) was named after Menes—the pharaoh who unified the two lands of upper and lower Kemet. Prior to the coming of the Greeks, the people called themselves Khamites and their country Kemet (ibid., 64-65).

3   Mrs. Durham was one of only a few thousand former African captives who were interviewed by the Federal Writers Project in order to describe her life and treatment during the Holocaust of Enslavement.

4   Both Green (1992) and Cole (1993) are correct to assign *Jumping the Broom* with ancient African origins. However, lacking concrete scholarly data to establish an African source of this custom, they rely heavily on antiquated explanations of a gypsy origin of this custom. There is also some basis to Green's attempts to attribute the origin of *Jumping the Broom* to Moors who populated the British Isles. However, the Moors were actually the last group of Africans to migrate to the isles of the North Atlantic. Commerce and cultural exchanges existed between the Moors and the Africans who resided in the British Isles prior to them. Hence, if the Moors performed broom weddings, they adopted this practice from their African predecessors.

5   Similar to many peoples of West Africa, the Scandinavians believed that the broom, or "thunder besom," was an implement of the gods. Although the Scandinavians did not jump the broom as part of their ceremony, they decorated the church and altar with branches of birch trees.

6   Kush was the high culture that existed north of Kemet from 3900 BCE to approximately 1400 CE.

7   The British peoples' conversions began in 596 CE when Augustine—most commonly called Austin—was sent to Brittany to convert the Germanic tribes to Christianity. While there, he became archbishop of Canterbury. According to Barashongo Ishakamusa, the archbishop (who was named after St. Augustine, the African, 354-430 CE) kept alive and disseminated culture and learning in Britain and mainland Europe during that continent's dark ages until the coming of the Moors.

8   The propagation of Christianity in the British Isles began in the fourth century CE.

9   Some of these deities experienced church-inflicted gender and/or role changes.

10   The goddess Brigid was a composite of many Kemetic goddesses—namely, Sekhmet, Bast, Het Heru, and Taweret.

11   Ptah is the self-created potter god, or "Master Builder," who shaped the world and heaven with the assistance of seven wise dwarfs of Khnemu. His tongue is identified with Djehuti, the god of writing and words. He is the husband of the goddess Sekhmet and is always symbolized carrying a staff that represents life, stability, and longevity.

12   The dragon was the emblem of the Nubian Grimaldi whose sojourn—according to Cheikh Anta Diop—in the British Isles can be traced back to approximately 30,000 BCE.

13   Many of the ancient noble families of the British Isles were Africans. Though many historians claim that the nobility of the British Isles were all white, a scrutiny of these families' insignias and coat-of-arms reveals that a significant number depicted themselves as black (Rogers 1967, 198-200).

14   The modern English word "passion," supposedly derives from the name "Pasch," one of the names for the Kemetic goddess Bast.

15   Het Heru was a major Kemetic goddess. The Greeks called her Hathor.

16   Tefnut and her twin brother/husband were the first deities to be created by Atum or Ra. Tefnut, who is often depicted as a lion-headed woman, is the personification of moisture, and Shu is the embodiment of the sky.

17   Septimus Severus, the black African emperor of Rome, oversaw the refurbishment Hadrian's Wall and upgrading of the mechanical defense systems throughout the British Isles in the second century CE. As commander and chief of the army, Severus, along with his officers and soldiers—who were also predominately black—spent a significant amount of time in Great Britain. Strains of these Africans' DNA have been detected in the people still living in proximity to this historic seventy-mile wall.

18   Nsibidi was an ideographical script that was used in West Africa as well as Kemet and throughout the central region of Africa to convey philosophical ideas and information. During the Ma'afa, Africans enslaved in the Americas also used this script. For example, nsibidi was woven into quilts and carved into objects—such as trees—to help to carefully guide Africans along the Underground Railroad and into the autonomous African settlements that existed in the American south.

19   Massey argues that, at times, the Scots were also called Cruitnich, or corn men, because the major crop they cultivated was corn.

20   Interestingly, according to some scholars, Halloween was originally celebrated as the Feast of Sekhmet and Bast.

21   The Iberians initially entered Spain under the headship of Batrikus, in 1000 BCE.

22   The worship of the goddess Sekhmet might have been introduced into Kemet by way of the Sudan. Sekhmet was originally a lion goddess, and lions were more plentiful in the Sudan than Kemet.

23   The Scottish practice of burying a container of dirt and alcohol completely mixed with the urine of the bride and groom to symbolize the union and indissolubility of their marriage is another example of a marital rite that can be traced to the Khoisan and Twa (T. W. Thompson 1969, 335).

24   The ash tree was also called the persea tree.

25　The Africans of the British Isles associated lightning with dragons and new beginnings.

26　Like Het Heru, Hera was also represented as a cow. Moreover, similar to Het Heru, she was the goddess of marriage and fertility.

27　Scant documentation exists concerning the practice of tree marriages in Telangana, India.

28　Nations of peoples such as the Asante, Ewe, Fon, Igbo, and Yoruba all believe that trees and their environs house sacred ancestors and other powerful spiritual entities. The Ewe people revere the silk-cotton tree as the abode of their god called Huntin. The Yoruba regard irokó trees as the homes of Irokó—the deity of abundance, fertility, and prosperity—and the Fon consider iroko trees (oak trees) to be incarnations of their ancestors. Likewise, Africans enslaved in the Americas, who hailed from various ethnic groups from western and southern Africa, believed that trees and mounds of earth above graves were at one with the spirits within these graves. They constructed bottle branches (also known as bottle trees) to harness this energy.

29　African dolls also denote marital commitment and are still used in some instances to convey newly married couples' desires to expeditiously conceive their firstborn child. The dolls used for the aforementioned purposes were usually made of wood, but they could also be made of natural fibers and other organic materials.

30　Before parading through the streets on horseback, the legendary Lady Godiva and successive females who engaged in this Godiva rite painted their bodies black. Moreover, Pliny, an ancient historian, stated that during religious festivals, the white women of ancient Briton painted their bodies black to resemble the color of Ethiopians (Spence 1949, 173).

31　The ancient Britons believed that the goddess Bast controlled the east, while Sekhmet was the goddess of the west. Among the Yoruba, the four deities charged with this function are Ogun (north), Obatala (south), Esu (east), and Sango (west). Ogun is the force of the north who controls earth and all metals. During the *Besom Wedding*, a bowl filled with dirt was used to represent him. Obatala is the force of the south who controls the depths of the ocean. The individual presiding over the ceremony would say, "May your love be as deep as the ocean." A container of water was used during the ceremony to represent Obatala. Esu, who is also associated with Shu, controls the east and the powers of air and wood. Şango is the passions of fire, and he controls the west.

32   Scholars' assumptions about the worship of Bes originating in central Africa stem from the title of "Lord of Punt," bestowed upon him by the Khamites. The first mention of Bes is in Pyramid Text number 1786. Devotees continued to pay homage to Bes until Constantine II suppressed his worship.

33   Some historians say that in earlier times, Bes was portrayed as being normal in height. In contrast to the other Kemetic gods, who are shown in profile, Bes is always depicted in full face with a large head, protruding tongue, bowlegs, and a bushy tail.

34   The Yoruba call good character "iwàpẹ̀lẹ́." According to the Yoruba, iwàpẹ̀lẹ́ is characterized by virtues such as respect, honesty, responsibility, cleanliness, morality, self-control, self-sufficiency, honor, and knowledge.

35   Massey argued that the ancient Britons adopted the use of sprigs of trees to communicate messages from the ancient Khamites. As ideographic writing pertains to Kemet, the goddess of writing, Seshat, for example, is pictured on temple and pyramid walls holding an ideograph made of a notched branch from the wood of a persea tree that she uses to record time as well as the deeds and reign of kings. Whereas Djehuti is credited with disseminating the art of writing, Seshat is credited with the creation of writing. According to Massey, the Irish word "beangan" and the Welsh word "pincen," for sprig or branch, are derivatives of the Kemetic word for ankh (ibid. 1994, 1:337). Lucas (1948) contends that the ideographic writing of the Yoruba can be interpreted through an examination of Kemetic hieroglyphics. It is my belief that the same can be said of the ideographic writing of enslaved and self-emancipated Africans in America.

36   Àròkó is an ideographic object script used to transmit from simple messages of a personal and practical nature to highly complex interpersonal messages. When these objects (called ideograms) are formed into simple shapes or elaborate configurations (called ideographs), they transmit ideas and feelings.

37   The number for six in the Yoruba language is *"efa." Efa* also means "I am drawn to you," from the verb *fa*, to draw. Mora is always implied as connected with *efa*: this means "stick to you, from the verb mo, to stick to, and the noun *ara*, or body, i.e., you.

38   Lucas (1970) states that any place or object to which palm leaves or fibers are tied becomes sacred (ibid., 162). According to the Yoruba, the world was created from sixteen branches of a sacred palm tree.

39   The number for six in the Yoruba language is "*efa.*" *Efa* also means "I am drawn to you,"
     from the verb *fa*, to draw. Mora is always implied as connected with efa and means "stick
     to you," from the verb mo, to stick to. The noun ara, body means "you." *Esan*, the
     Yoruba word for nine, also means the "rewards or benefits will be great". If the woman
     was somewhat interested but needed time to make up her mind she would send back
     three pieces of broom wrapped in a palm leaf. The Yoruba word for three is "eta." Eta,
     from the word motanu, means I have sent it back. Eta also means "deceit." This message
     indicates that the woman was not sure that the man would be faithful.

40   According to Lucas (1948), the Yoruba also pays tribute to Het Heru for her function
     in the creation of male semen. Lucas argues the Yoruba name for semen, "Ato," is
     derived from this goddess's Greek name.

41   Ra is a very old solar god who has the power to create and destroy. He represents life,
     rebirth, children, health and virility. He was a major deity throughout ancient Kemet.

42   Ma'at is ethical principles collectively representing the values of truth, justice, harmony,
     balance, cosmological order, reciprocity, and propriety. According to the Khamites,
     without Ma'at, disorder and chaos would prevail and all of creation would perish.
     Ma'at is personified as a woman wearing a tall ostrich feather on top her head. Ma'at
     is the daughter of the god Ra.

43   For those who died of smallpox, the elaborate burial rites and traditional celebration
     that normally followed had to be omitted. Deceased persons diagnosed with this
     infection could not be buried on the family compound, instead special undertakers
     had to do the embalming, and their bodies were carried away and disposed of in the
     forests (Idowu 1962, 98).

44   Although the Khamites most notably depicted Shu as a man holding a single ostrich
     feather, symbolically, in a similar manner, at times, they represented him—as well as
     the element of air—as a block of wood. A club made of wood was also used to
     represent Sòpònná.

45   The *alàwiyè* is the name given to the person whose duty it is to orally recite the
     history and edicts of the Yoruba people. The *alàwiyè* is charged with making certain
     that what is being uttered is true and fully understood by the recipients of the
     message and information. In Yoruba, *alà* literally means "someone who translates for
     an audience." *Wi* means to "tell," and *yè* means "to make understood."

46   *The Book of Don'ts* is a record of established taboos that were, at one time, meticulously followed by the Yoruba to help to preserve the health and well-being of the entire nation.

47   Oak trees were also deemed sacred and were oftentimes used to make the besoms used in the *Jumping the Broom* ceremony. Oak trees also held great significance to the Druids. It was in the groves of these trees where their sacred ceremonies were conducted.

48   The Puritans attacked the Maypole, calling it "a heathenish vanity greatly abused to superstition and wickedness" (Philpot 1994/1897, 21).

49   Red, white, and black are also the colors of the goddesses Brigid and Ma'at.

50   The Yoruba call the power housed in the color red as "asé."

51   Among many African peoples (i.e., the Bambara, Ewe, Khamites, and Yoruba) the vulture, in particular, and birds, in general, are symbols of motherhood. The Kemetic goddess Mut was represented as a vulture. Furthermore, the Ewe goddess Aizan, the Yoruba goddess Oya, and the Bambara goddess Nyale all preside over wind, lightning, numerous bodies of water, and are the West African equivalents of Nekhebet.

52   Neith, whom Morrigan is fashioned from, was always depicted as a woman. However, she was linked with masculine concerns of war and hunting and was often depicted carrying a bow and arrow (Tyldesley 1994, 254).

53   The lotus flower, which opens its petals at daybreak and closes them at night, was associated with the daily rebirth of Ra—the sun god—and by extension was symbolic of rebirth after death.

54   The Afro-Britons believed that burials under sycamore trees and in sycamore coffins—in a fetal position—were symbolic of the return to the womb of the tree goddesses Auset, Het Heru, and Nut. They believed, moreover, that Ra or Re, the sun god, emerged every day from the sycamore tree. The wood is impervious to water and was used extensively by the African Britons to make agricultural implements and for building ships. The sycamore is not indigenous to the British Isles, and it does not reproduce itself. A branch must be broken off and planted. The sycamore tree was imported from southern Africa.

INDEX

www.ingramcontent.com/pod-product-compliance
Lightning Source LLC
Chambersburg PA
CBHW020401290526
45785CB00005B/2393